SOU

The
Spanda Karikas

RANJIT CHAUDHRI

Reprint 2023

FiNGERPRINT!
An imprint of Prakash Books India Pvt. Ltd

113/A, Darya Ganj,
New Delhi-110 002
Email: info@prakashbooks.com/sales@prakashbooks.com

facebook www.facebook.com/fingerprintpublishing
twitter www.twitter.com/FingerprintP
www.fingerprintpublishing.com

ISBN: 978 93 5440 170 1

Processed & printed in India

CONTENTS

INTRODUCTION

The *Spanda Karikas* was written by the sage Vasugupta in the late 8th, or early 9th century AD. Vasugupta is known for the *Shiva Sutras*, a text revealed to him by Lord Shiva.

The *Spanda Karikas* beautifully explains some of the subject matter of the *Shiva Sutras.* It also covers entirely new areas. At places, the wisdom it contains is breathtaking.

What does *Spanda Karikas* mean? Spanda literally means vibration, throb, pulse, or movement. In this system, it has a larger meaning. Spanda stands for pure consciousness, Divine consciousness, or the highest form of consciousness. It is the state of Shiva or God. It is not inert, passive consciousness. It is a dynamic, vibrant, pulsating consciousness, which is throbbing with life. This consciousness is the creator of the universe and of all forms in it. It is the seed of all life forms. This is consciousness with a divine pulse or throb within it. Hence, the word Spanda has been used to describe Divine consciousness. It contains within it a certain dynamism or energy.

Most mystics describe our highest state to be that of pure consciousness. Vasugupta agrees with that. However, he gives consciousness a new name, Spanda, to describe it more accurately. Consciousness is not passive; it is dynamic. It contains an energy or life force within it that is responsible for all creation.

Karikas, according to the *Sanskrit-English Dictionary* by Monier Monier-Williams means, "Concise statement in verse of philosophical and grammatical doctrine." *Spanda Karikas* literally means verses on the doctrine of Spanda, or verses on the subject matter of Divine pulsating consciousness.

The *Spanda Karikas* and the *Shiva Sutras* belong to the Spanda School of Kashmir Shaivism, which is one of four schools of thought in Kashmir Shaivism. Two other important texts of this school are the *Vigyan Bhairava Tantra* and the *Paratrishika.*

Kashmir Shaivism is a philosophy that is non-dualistic. It teaches that there is not two, but only One. We are not separate from our Creator, but one with it. Only God exists. Everything and everyone is part of God. There is no separation between the Creator and the created. God, or the Supreme Being, in this philosophy is called *Param* Shiva (Supreme Shiva), or sometimes simply Shiva. The process of realising our oneness with God is called self-realisation or liberation. We realise our true self, and our true self is Shiva or God.

There are ancient commentaries on the *Spanda Karikas*—by Kallata, Ramakantha, Bhatta Utpala, and Kshemaraja. The verses used here are taken from Kshemaraja's work. Traditionally, the *Spanda Karikas* contained 52 verses. Kshemaraja's text has 53. He has added one more verse, explaining the benefits of the knowledge contained in this text.

Most commentaries have divided the text into three or four chapters. However, it is a short text and was meant to be read at one stretch. I have kept all the verses in one chapter. At the end of the book, the verses are repeated without any commentary, for the benefit of those who wish to read the original text, without any break or commentary.

The *Spanda Karikas* contains a wealth of knowledge. It explains to us how the world has been created, what are the important elements within it, what causes our bondage, and the means to overcome our bondage. Like all great texts, the *Spanda Karikas* is transformative. Its verses can transform our life, and take us to a higher plane of existence. Drink from its cup of wisdom, and watch your life transform.

Spanda Karikas

1

Yasyonmeṣanimeṣābhyāṃ jagataḥ pralayodayau/
Taṃ Sakticakravibhaprabhavaṃ Śaṅkaraṃ stumaḥ//

We praise that Shiva, who is the source of all energy existing everywhere, and by whose opening and closing of eyes, the universe is created or destroyed.

In Kashmir Shaivism, Lord Shiva is the highest reality. He is the Supreme Being, God, and the Ultimate Truth. However, it is important to understand that he is the *only reality*. Only Lord Shiva or God exists. We are all part of him. All energy everywhere is only Shiva's energy. All matter is created by God's energy, which is why we are always part of God, and never apart from God. Our journey towards Self-Realisation is to realise and experience this truth—our eternal oneness with God.

Lord Shiva is sometimes depicted as *ardhnariswara*, half male, half female. This is to show that both male and female principles unite in him, and he is neither male nor female. Intuitively, we also know that God is neither male nor female.

Most Shiva temples have a bowl shaped like a woman's cervix with a *lingam*, representing the male sexual organ, springing out from the middle of it. This is to show that male and female energies are united in Lord Shiva. In Shaivism, one of the holiest places of pilgrimage is Mount Kailash, where Lord Shiva is said to reside. Mount Kailash is in present-day Tibet. It is shaped like a *lingam*. The lingam arises from the base of the mountain, which is shaped like a cervix. Mount Kailash is a natural formation, showing the unity of the male and female principles. Most Shiva temples try to replicate this natural formation.

The universe is created, maintained, and destroyed by Lord Shiva. When Shiva's eyes are open, the universe is being created. When his eyes are half-open, the universe cycle is in process, and the universe is being maintained. Finally, when Shiva's eyes are closed, the universe is being dissolved.

2

Yatra sthitam idaṃ sarvaṃ kāryaṃ yasmācca nirgatam/
Tasyānāvṛtarūpatvān na nirodho 'sti kutracit//

In whom this whole world rests and from whom
it has come, cannot be restrained anywhere,
as its nature is open.

The whole world rests and emanates from Shiva. The nature of Shiva or God cannot be concealed or covered because the very nature of God is to be free, unrestrained, and visible. The Creator cannot be hidden as the imprint of the Creator lies in everything. The very nature of God is to be free and unrestrained. The illusion tries to conceal God's nature, but if you look carefully, and see past the illusion, you will find God.

What exactly is God's nature? God's nature is consciousness. The very first sutra of the *Shiva Sutras* says that the Self is consciousness. The ability to be conscious or self-aware exists in every human being. Other forms of existence, such as plant and animal life, do not have the ability to be self-aware. For this reason, human life is a blessing. We have the potential to reach our highest state, a state of full awareness or oneness with God. Other life forms with lower consciousness do not have this potential.

On the other hand, human life can also be challenging. This is because we have a mind, and our mind causes suffering. Certain events in our life may disturb us and cause us pain. But pain does not have to cause suffering. It is our thoughts about that event that causes suffering. Our mind judges that event, calls it negative, and causes suffering. We think, "This is wrong, this should not be happening to me, how unfairly I am being treated," and so on. When we continue to delve in negative thoughts, we remain disturbed. Buddha taught that a person who continuously thinks, "He abused me, he beat me, he robbed me, he defeated me," pain follows him night and day. On the contrary, a person who does not think, "He abused me, he beat me, he robbed me, he defeated me" (even though he was abused, beaten, robbed or defeated), happiness follows him night and day.

Therefore, humans have the ability to experience two extremes—suffering because of the mind, and our highest state through consciousness. Lower forms of existence do not have a mind and, thus, do not suffer like humans. At the same time, due to their lower level of consciousness, they do not have the ability to experience oneness with God.

3

Jāgradādivibhede 'pi tadabhinne prasarpati/
Nivartate nijānnaiva svabhāvādupalabdhṛtaḥ//

That which is undivided extends even into the division appearing in the waking state, etc. because one who is aware does not leave their own natural state.

That which is undivided is God. God extends even into the division appearing in the waking state, or the dream state. In the waking state and the dream state, we experience many different objects and life forms. Each object has a boundary, and looks different from other objects. This division is apparent to all of us in the waking state as well as dream state.

What is not apparent is how these objects are formed. As explained later in the text, all objects are formed by consciousness. God is pure consciousness. Objects may be many but consciousness is one. Every object in its essence is only consciousness. Therefore, God or consciousness extends even into the division appearing in the waking state and dream state.

One who is aware does not leave their own natural state of consciousness. In a state of awareness, there is a certain disconnect with the body. One ceases to identify with the body. At higher levels of awareness, there is an increased feeling of unity with other objects. At the level of full awareness, one experiences no separation whatsoever. There is a story in Buddha's life to illustrate this. Once, he was invited to go hunting with his relatives. One of his relatives shot a bird with his arrow. The bird fell to the ground in pain. Buddha cried out in anguish, and rushed toward the bird. At his level of consciousness, Buddha experienced the pain the bird was experiencing. This story is trying to convey a message. Ultimately, we are all one.

4

Ahaṃ sukhī ca duḥkhī ca raktaśca ityādisamvidaḥ/
Sukhādyavasthānusyūte vartante 'nyatra tāḥ sphuṭam//

"I am happy, I am pained, I am satisfied." These and other feelings evidently abide in another place, where the states of pleasure, pain, etc. are strung together.

Feelings of pleasure, pain, greed, anger, lust, and other emotions are experienced by all human beings at some point in time in their lives. In Hinduism, the way to overcome negative emotions is not through suppression but by elevating our awareness. When we feel anger, we lose our awareness. It is impossible to be angry when one is aware. Becoming angry means that we have lost ourselves completely in the situation, and we have no self-awareness at that point of time.

When our awareness levels rise, our feelings of anger, lust, greed, suffering, etc. automatically diminish. After a certain point, these emotions vanish completely.

Our feelings of pain and pleasure also arise because of our strong identification with the body. The body experiences both pain and pleasure. In a heightened state of awareness, one ceases to identify with the body. Next, as the *Shiva Sutras* state, pleasure and pain are experienced as something external. It seems to be happening to someone else, not to you. There are stories of masters who have died of cancer. They should have been experiencing pain while suffering from cancer, but they experienced none of it. This was because they had reached a state where they no longer identified with the body, and what was happening to the body no longer affected them.

These and other feelings evidently abide in another place, where the feelings of pleasure, pain, etc. are strung together. These and other feelings abide in a place called unconsciousness. This is a state where we are awake, but there is no awareness.

5

Na duḥkhaṃ na sukhaṃ yatra na grāhyaṃ grāhakaṃ na ca/
Na cāsti mūḍhabhāvo 'pi tadasti paramārthataḥ//

Where there is neither pain nor pleasure, neither object nor subject, and nor is there also unconsciousness, that is the highest truth.

The highest truth is that there is only one. There is neither object nor subject. Pleasure and pain, and other feelings associated with the body, are absent. There is also no unconsciousness. Unconsciousness here refers to the state of deep sleep. In deep sleep, there are no dreams, no objects or subject, and nor are there any feelings of pleasure or pain. However, the state of deep sleep is different from the state of enlightenment. In the enlightened state, there is full awareness. In deep sleep or unconsciousness, there is no awareness.

The masters of Kashmir Shaivism explained that we either see Divine Reality or we see the world. We either experience Divinity or we experience the illusion. The illusion shows separation, subject and object, and pleasure and pain. After enlightenment, there is no pleasure or pain, only bliss. There is no separation, or subject and object, there is only one. There is a term that is used to describe enlightenment—*Kevala.* Kevala means there is only One and the One is alone. After enlightenment, the realisation dawns that only you exist. You are one with God, and nothing other than God exists.

6

**Yataḥ karaṇa-vargo 'yaṃ vimūḍho 'mūḍhavat svayam/
Sahāntareṇa cakreṇa pravṛtti-sthiti-saṃhṛtīḥ//**

From where does this group of sense organs, along with the inner chakras that are lifeless, become conscious of their own, and what is responsible for their creation, maintenance, and destruction?

What breathes life into the body? The sense organs and the rest of the body are controlled by the inner chakras. A chakra literally means wheel. It is a wheel of energy or an energy centre. There are seven important chakras. The chakras, along with energy pathways (*nadis*), form the subtle body, according to the physiology of yoga. The subtle body or energy body controls our gross body.

The sense organs and the rest of the gross body, along with the chakras and energy system, are initially lifeless. So, what gives them life and makes them conscious? What element is responsible for their creation, maintenance, and destruction?

Vasugupta gives the answer in verse 12. It is consciousness that gives life to our gross body and to the chakras. Consciousness is our Soul or our Self. It is sometimes referred to as the casual body. The physiology of the human body, according to yoga, is something like this: on the surface we have the gross body. This is the body we are aware of. Controlling the gross body is the energy body or the subtle body, comprising of the chakras and energy pathways. Finally, beyond the energy body, we have our soul or our Self, called the causal body. The casual body or our soul is consciousness. Consciousness gives life to our energy body and to our gross body.

Medical science only recognises the gross body. This is because if you cut up the human body, you will not find any chakras, nor will you find your soul. However, yoga says that chakras do exist. They are not gross but subtle in nature, which is why you cannot see them with the naked eye. There are some yogic practices that control and stimulate some of the chakras. For example, the root chakra is *Mooladhara* chakra, located at the base of the body. In men, it is located at the perineum between the male sexual organ and the anus. In women, it is situated in the region of the cervix. Our dormant energy, *Kundalini*, is said to be located at Mooladhara chakra. Mooladhara is responsible for our sexual energy, amongst other things. Certain yogic practices, such as *Siddhasana* and *Moola Bandha*, seek to control and convert sexual energy for spiritual purposes. They seek to curb our sexual instinct and bring it into balance, so that we are focused more on our spiritual growth than on pleasures of the flesh. Most illnesses are caused because our energy body goes out of balance.

Ancient eastern forms of healing view the body holistically and seek to cure illnesses by bringing the energy system back into harmony.

7

Labhate tatprayatnena parīkṣyaṃ tattvam ādarāt/
Yataḥ svatantratā tasya sarvatreyam akṛtrimā//

One should examine carefully with effort, and grasp that element, which by virtue of its natural freedom existing everywhere, is responsible for this.

The element referred to here is consciousness. Vasugupta gave consciousness a new name: he called it Spanda. He did so to define it better. Spanda literally means vibration, movement, pulse, or throb. Consciousness has a certain vibration or throb within it. Consciousness is not passive, it is dynamic. It is pregnant with energy and with the throb of life.

In Kashmir Shaivism, the example of the fish, *Matsyodari*, is given. Outwardly, the fish may be still, but inwardly the belly of the fish keeps throbbing. This is the basic signature of consciousness. Outwardly, there may or may not be movement, but inwardly there is a throb or vibration. The basic pattern of consciousness is found everywhere. This verse and verse 2 states that the nature of consciousness is freedom, and to be visible. Consciousness cannot be restrained or concealed anywhere.

Vasugupta says that this particular quality of consciousness, which he called Spanda, is found everywhere in the external world. Everything has some movement, throb, or vibration. If you examine an inert object like a table or a rock, it will seem on the surface that there is no movement. However, the subatomic particles are always in movement. All matter at its minutest level is composed of atoms. Atoms themselves are composed of sub-atomic particles called protons, neutrons, and electrons. The protons and neutrons form a nucleus, and the electrons constantly move around the nucleus in a particular orbit. The protons and neutrons are further composed of smaller matter called quarks, anti-quarks, and gluons. These quarks, anti-quarks, and gluons are constantly in motion. Therefore, at the smallest level, there is always some movement. A table may be still on the surface, but within it, there is always some movement, at the sub-atomic level.

Most of what we know about sub-atomic particles was discovered in the 20th century, mainly in the 1970s and 1980s. Vasugupta was writing about this movement in the 8th century AD, a full 12 centuries before modern physics discovered the truth of what he was saying.

The verse says one should grasp that element. The element is consciousness, and one should grasp consciousness. This basically means that one should be conscious, one should be aware. This is explained in further detail in the next few verses.

8

Na hīcchānodanasyāyaṃ prerakatvena vartate/
Api tvātmabalasparśāt puruṣastatsamo bhavet//

An individual cannot set a desire in motion on their own. But only by being in contact with the power of the Self, one is able to do this. One should become identical to the Self.

In Hinduism, the soul and the Self are the same. Normally, all our attention is directed outwards. When we redirect some of our attention back towards ourselves, we become a witness. We are then in a state of awareness and we observe all the events in our life. This witness is our Self. It is pure consciousness. The Self or consciousness is everything. One of the most important pieces of spiritual advice can be summed up in three words—"Be a witness."

When we redirect our attention back towards ourselves, we become self-aware, and that profoundly changes the quality of our life. This verse stresses the power of the Self in achieving a desire. The Self or consciousness is Shiva or God. It is what breathes life into our body. It is also the creator of all forms in the universe. It is literally the power that makes the world go round. We are able to achieve anything worthwhile only because of the power of the Self. Without the Self, we are nothing.

One should become identical to the Self. One should constantly be aware and should identify with consciousness, not with the body. If the Self is everything, then one should focus on the Self, not on the external world. Our attention should be directed towards the Creator of the external world, not on what has been created. Ramana Maharshi used to teach that there is one power (the Self) that is responsible for all that we see, and for the act of seeing them. One should focus on That," he said. Become identical to the Self, as the verse says.

9

Nijāśuddhyāsamarthasya kartavyeṣv abhilāṣiṇaḥ/
Yadā kṣobhaḥ pralīyeta tadā syāt paramaṃ padam//

An individual is incapable of fulfilling their desires because of their impurities. When the agitation of the mind ceases, then one will enter the Highest State.

There are three impurities that stand in the way of us experiencing our true nature. The first and main impurity is *Aanava.* Aanava literally means minute. It is the impurity of ignorance. Due to ignorance, we are unable to experience our highest state, and believe we are the body. Our body is something infinitesimally small compared to our real Self, which is infinite. That is why the term Aanava has been used. Ignorance causes us to believe we are the body and not the Self.

The second impurity is *Maayiya.* Maayiya means proceeding from the illusion. The illusion conceals our true nature. The illusory world we live in reinforces our identification with our body and our feeling of separateness. We see many different people and forms, who look separate and different from us and that makes us believe we are the body, different and separate from everyone else.

The third impurity is *Karma.* It proceeds from the earlier two impurities. Karma makes us believe we are the doer—we are the one doing things. In reality, we are the witness, the Self. The body does things, not our real Self. Our real Self only observes.

The way to remove our impurities and reach our highest state is to still the mind. The previous two verses exhorted us to be aware, be conscious, and to identify with the Self. What prevents us from being aware? Our active mind prevents us from being in a state of awareness. When we are thinking, we cannot be aware. Thoughts cause us to lose awareness. One of the most important texts of this school of Kashmir Shaivism is the *Vigyan Bhairava Tantra.* In verse 15 of the text, Lord Shiva says we reach our highest state when the mind is still and free of thoughts. He then proceeds to give 112 meditations to still the mind.

The verse uses the word 'agitation.' The agitation is of the mind. The mind becomes agitated when our attention goes outward to the world. We will not find sustaining peace in the world. The world will disturb us. We only find peace when our attention is focused inwards on the Self. Ramana Maharshi used to teach that when we focus our attention on the external world, we experience pain; when we direct it inwards to the Self, we experience peace.

10

Tadāsyākṛtrimo dharmo jñatvakartṛtvalakṣaṇaḥ/
Yatas tadepsitaṃ sarvaṃ jānāti ca karoti ca//

Then the real nature of this one is established, whose very quality is knowledge and activity. Due to this, one is then able to know and do everything one desires.

In our highest state, we become one with God. God's intrinsic quality is to be all-knowing and all-powerful. God knows everything and can do anything. An enlightened person is one with God and becomes God in human form. Consequently, they are able to know or do anything they desire.

The previous verse said that an unenlightened person has difficulty in fulfilling their desires because of their impurities. After enlightenment, all barriers are removed. One's basic nature is to be omniscient and all-powerful. One can then accomplish anything they desire. Desires are fulfilled immediately. They do not take long to materialise. In an unenlightened state, desires may take long to fructify. As we grow in our awareness, our desires start materialising faster. After enlightenment, desires are fulfilled instantaneously.

11

Tam adhiṣṭhātṛbhāvena svabhāvam avalokayan/
Smayamāna ivāste yastasyeyaṃ kusṛtiḥ kutaḥ//

How can he, who looks with astonishment at his natural state, which presides over everything, continue in this selfish way?

In the liberated state, there is no ego. There is no trace of the individual. It is, therefore, impossible to have selfish desires. One becomes all-knowing and all-powerful only when it becomes impossible to misuse this knowledge and power. Misuse only arises when there is an ego. With an ego we may desire to earn money, achieve certain goals, or even harm somebody. Without an ego, one only works for the common good. In the highest state, you cannot work for your individual self because there is no individual left. In that elevated state, one can materialise desires immediately. But the irony is that there are no selfish desires left that one wishes to materialise. "How can one continue in this selfish way?" the verse asks.

12

Nābhāvo bhāvyatāmeti na ca tatrāsty amūḍhatā/
Yato 'bhiyoga-saṃsparśāt tadāsid iti niścayaḥ//

Non-existence cannot be the state of being to strive for, as there is no consciousness and no existence there. Only from being in constant contact with consciousness can there be existence. This is for certain.

Certain philosophical systems prevailing in Kashmir in the 8th century AD used to teach that non-existence was the highest state. This verse is refuting them. Non-existence cannot be the ultimate state, as there is no existence there. The highest state must have existence. Without existence, there is nothing of value.

Only from being in constant contact with consciousness can there be existence. The question raised in verses 6 and 7 is finally answered here. What breathes life into our body? The answer is consciousness. All matter is created by consciousness. Without consciousness, there can be no existence. At some level, we are constantly in touch with our consciousness. When consciousness decides to leave our body, our body dies.

The verse emphatically says that without consciousness, there can be no existence and this is for certain. Consciousness is another name for God. God is pure consciousness. If you substitute God for consciousness in the above verse, you may find it easier to understand. "Non-existence cannot be the state of being to strive for, as there is no God and no existence there. Only from being in constant contact with God can there be existence. This is for certain."

Later, this text explains that other than the waking state and the dream state, God appears as pure consciousness.

13

Atastatkṛtrimaṃ jñeyaṃ sauṣupta-padavat sadā/
Na tvevaṃ smaryamāṇatvaṃ tat tattvaṃ pratipadyate//

For this reason that artificial state is to be understood as similar to being continuously in deep sleep. However, the real state is not remembered as occurring in this way.

Non-existence is an artificial state. It is similar to deep sleep because in deep sleep there is also no consciousness. We are not aware that we exist. The real state is completely different. It is a state of full awareness. We are aware and we are aware of our sense of awareness. "I am that I am," as the Bible states so cryptically.

The thought or the feeling *I am* is very powerful. It is a practice that can liberate us. The feeling *I am* causes us to focus on the Being or the Self within us that exists.

Sri Nisargadatta Maharaj was one of India's greatest sages of the 20th century. His wisdom manifests clearly in conversations with his disciples, which are published in the book, *I Am That: Talks with Sri Nisargadatta Maharaj*. In response to a question, he describes how he came to be enlightened. His teacher told him to hold on to the sense, "I am," tenaciously. He did so and found that this brought an end to his mind. In the stillness of his mind, he reached the highest state.

I am makes us realise there is a Self or a witness within us. A Being far greater than the body, which is unbound and eternal.

14

Avasthāyugalaṃ cātra kāryakartṛtva-śabditam/
Kāryatā kṣayiṇī tatra kartṛtvaṃ punarakṣayam//

Two are found to exist here, called the Creator and the created. Among them, created matter is subject to decay but the Creator is imperishable.

The next three verses are beautiful. They remove our fear of death and of change. Two are found to exist here, the Creator and created matter. Created matter has been created by the Creator. Our entire universe is created matter. All created matter is subject to change, decay, and death. Only the Creator is eternal.

The process of change can sometimes disturb us. The midlife crisis some people go through in their forties is a result of coming face to face with their mortality. After we turn 40, the health and fitness of our body declines. The first thing that goes is our eyesight. We find it difficult to focus on objects near us and usually require reading glasses. This is a result of the muscles in our eyes that control our lenses, becoming weaker. Faced with declining health, we realise our bodies are not going to live forever. We understand that we, too, have an expiry date. We then look back at our life and question whether we have achieved what we had set out to, and whether our lives are going in the direction we want it to. This questioning can occasionally trigger a midlife crisis.

Sometimes a simple incident can bring you face to face with your mortality. My moment of realisation came shortly after I turned 40. I had gone to see my doctor because of a throat ailment. She asked me how old I was. I said I had just turned 40. She jokingly replied, "It's all downhill from here." Her answer startled me and stirred something within me. Up to that time, I had been practicing yoga regularly and had kept myself fairly fit. I had suffered no major health issues. But suddenly I realised no matter what I did, my health was slowly going to decline, and I was going to face more and more health issues.

So how does one handle change and the decay of our bodies? The answer is given in the next two verses.

15

Kāryonmukhaḥ prayatno yaḥ kevalaṃ so 'tra lupyate/
Tasmiṃl lupte vilupto 'smītyabudhaḥ pratipadyate//

Looking at created matter dissolving into the Whole, examine carefully what is being destroyed here. At the time of his death, an ignorant man thinks, "I will cease to exist."

When we see created matter decaying and dissolving into the Whole, what is actually being destroyed? When our bodies start ageing and dying, examine carefully what is being destroyed. It is our bodies, of course. But we are not our body, we are our soul. It is the identification with our body that causes fear of death. Death happens to our body, not to our real self. When we understand this, we lose our fear of death. We then see death as the stripping away of our body, as we do when we replace an old garment with a new one. This was the example given by Lord Krishna in the *Bhagavad Gita*. The body is a cover, like a garment. Death is the removal of the cover, like the removal of an old garment.

A larger principle also needs to be accepted here. All created matter is subject to change, decay, and death. This is a natural process that cannot be stopped. We sometimes suffer when we refuse to accept this process. There are some who feel disturbed by the ageing process and the loss of one's looks; they seek to reverse it through various beauty treatments. However, this does not bring lasting peace or happiness. Peace is only achieved when we understand that this is a natural process that happens to all created matter, and that nothing real or of any significance is being destroyed. The *Ashtavakra Gita* explains it beautifully (11.1):

All things arise,
experience change
and pass away.

This is their inherent nature.

When you understand this,
you remain unperturbed
and free from pain.

Through this peace in fact,
you become still.

16

Na tu yo 'ntarmukho bhāvaḥ sarvajñatva-guṇāspadam/
Tasya lopaḥ kadācitsyād anyasyānupalambhanāt//

But the Being within us, who is the abode of the quality of omniscience, cannot be destroyed. Due to lack of knowledge of his other Self, a man believes, sooner or later, he may cease to exist.

The Being within us is eternal; it is the Creator. It is not subject to change or decay. It cannot be destroyed. When we identify with our body, we forget about this Being, our witnessing Self or our Soul. When we see our body dying, we mistakenly believe that our life will end with our body. However, our body is not our real self. Our soul is our real self and it is eternal. Nisargadatta Maharaj explained this beautifully to a disciple: "Once you know that death happens to the body and not to you, you just watch your body falling off like a discarded garment. The real you is timeless and beyond birth and death. The body will survive as long as it is needed. It is not important that it should last long."

There are two meditations given in the *Vigyan Bhairava Tantra* that help us grasp the important truth contained in the last three verses. Verses 52 and 53 state:

Imagine one's own body being burnt by a destructive fire, rising from the right foot to the top. Then one will attain a calm splendour.

Similarly, meditate with undivided attention, that the entire world is burnt by fire. That person then attains the highest state.

When we practice these two meditations, we realise that even when our body, or the entire world, is destroyed, we are still here. We are now awareness or consciousness, and consciousness does not need a body to survive. In fact, it is our body that needs consciousness to survive, not the other way around. There are two important messages being given here: even when our body is destroyed, we still exist; and our real self is consciousness.

What these practices do is remove our fear of death. When we are not scared of dying, then we are not scared of living. For the first time, we can live our life fearlessly.

When we realise we live forever; we face our day-to-day problems in an entirely new way. How significant can any of our problems be, when we understand we are eternal? When the entire world with everything in it is destroyed, we will still survive. With this understanding, our perception of our daily problems and life's challenges changes completely. They appear so insignificant compared to the vastness of our true nature. We no longer allow them to disturb our peace and live our life in an entirely new way.

17

Tasyopalabdhiḥ satataṃ tripadāvyabhicāriṇī/
Nityaṃ syāt suprabuddhasya tadādyante parasya tu//

A fully enlightened person is constantly aware of his Self in the three transitory states. But others may find their Being at the beginning and end of these states.

A liberated person is constantly aware. There is no break in their awareness. Their awareness continues in all the three states—the waking state, the dream state, and the state of deep sleep. An enlightened person is actually in a fourth state—the state of super-consciousness. This fourth state is sometimes called *turiya.* It is a state of full awareness and complete self-realisation. In this state, even while sleeping, an enlightened person is always aware of the Self.

But others may find their Being at the beginning and end of these states. What is special about the beginning or end of these three states? At the beginning or end of the waking state, the dream state, or the state of deep sleep, the possibility of entering the fourth state of full consciousness exists. When we are crossing over from one state of consciousness to the next, the potential to reach enlightenment is there. However, we cannot seize this potential during the dream state and state of deep sleep. When we are sleeping, we have no awareness, and we cannot identify the beginning and end of these states. It is only possible to practice this when we are awake and slowly drifting to sleep. Verse 75 of the *Vigyan Bhairava Tantra* explains:

Concentrate on the state where sleep has not fully appeared, but the external world has disappeared. In that state, the Supreme Goddess is revealed.

As we are drifting to sleep, we have to maintain some semblance of awareness. This is the time when the waking state is ending and the sleep state is beginning. We have to be careful. If we are fully aware, we will be fully awake, and we will not experience the end of the waking state. A delicate balance has to be maintained between being aware and trying to sleep. If we are successful, we will suddenly slip into the fourth state of super consciousness, and gain enlightenment.

18

Jñānajñeya-svarūpiṇyā śaktyā paramayā yutaḥ/
Padadvaye vibhurbhāti tadanyatra tu cinmayaḥ//

The all-pervading Lord, through the supreme power he possesses, appears in the form of knowledge and objects of knowledge, in the waking state and dream state. But other than these states, God appears as pure Consciousness.

Form of knowledge and objects of knowledge refer to the different forms and objects we see during the waking state and dream state. Some of these may be animate and some may be inanimate. God appears as various forms and objects during the waking and dream states. However, other than these two states, God only appears as pure Consciousness, and does not take any other form or shape.

What all this means is that forms are not the essence of God. The essence of God is consciousness. The words God and pure Consciousness are interchangeable. Does this mean that we should not worship God in any form? No, we are free to worship God in any form. Any aspect of Divinity can be used as a portal for entering the Divine. That is why Hinduism has over 30 million gods and goddesses. They cater to our individual needs and preferences. Some people may find a particular tree sacred. Others may find a particular rock sacred and find that worshipping that rock takes them closer to God. The beauty about Tantra and Hinduism is that they allow us to worship any form of God that we find appealing, and that enables us to discover our own Divinity. The entire world is nothing but a manifestation of the Divine. We are free to worship any aspect of it that we find sacred and that helps us reach God.

19

Guṇādispandaniṣyandāḥ sāmānyaspandasaṃśrayāt/
Labdhātmalābhāḥ satataṃ syur Jñasyāparipanthinaḥ//

Creation of matter, beginning with the qualities, issues from vibration that is connected to the universal vibration of Consciousness. From not standing in the way of knowing this, people may be able to permanently realise their true Self.

For the first time in the text, the word *Spanda* has been used. It has been translated as vibration in the above verse. Matter is created by the elements of creation. There are 36 elements of creation. The theory of creation in Tantra is discussed extensively in other texts. The *Shiva Sutras* also touches on it.

The above verse refers to the qualities. There are three qualities—*tamas* (inertia), *rajas* (motion or activity), and *sattva* (balance or illumination). These three qualities are part of nature (*prakriti*), the 13th element of creation, and are one of the important elements responsible for the creation of gross matter.

Nature and its three qualities are created by vibrations that are connected to the vibration of consciousness. In effect, nature, its qualities, and all matter are created by consciousness. Consciousness is the Creator and all matter is created by it.

Today, our scientists are telling us that all matter is created by vibration of energies. This is something that this text told us centuries ago.

From not standing in the way of knowing this, people may be able to permanently realise their true Self. When we understand the truth, that all matter is only a form of consciousness, we are able to look past the illusion and not get entrapped by it. We understand that we are all one, and the illusion we are seeing is not real. We recognise the Divinity within each form and every form, in essence, is consciousness. This truth is summarised by the famous Indian greeting, *Namaste*, which means, "God in me honours God in you."

Realising everything is only consciousness extinguishes the desire for material objects. Desire can bind us. As the *Shiva Sutras* explains (3:40):

Due to desire moving outwards for external objects, an individual is carried from life to life.

When you realise that everything is made of the same thing (consciousness), you will stop desiring it. Normally, we value objects differently, based on their usefulness to us, and its monetary value. Objects of greater economic worth, such as gold, are given greater value than objects of less economic worth. However, understanding that everything is only consciousness changes our perception completely. Every object is given equal value because it is composed of the same thing. We are able to look through the illusion and see the essence of every object, not just its form. The essence of everything is the same. This change in perception liberates us.

20

Aprabudhadhiyas tvete svasthitisthaganodyatāḥ/
Pātayanti duruttāre ghore saṃsāra-vartmani//

However, these created matter are active in concealing one's true state and cause the unawakened to fall into the painful path of world illusion, which is difficult to overcome.

Created matter conceals our true state by bringing forth the illusion of separateness. Each object appears to be separate from other objects. This causes us to identify with our own form, believing that it is finite and separate from other objects. Due to identification with form, there is fear of death. Due to a feeling of separation, the desire for other objects arises. Separation can also give rise to feelings of competition, fear, and hatred. Since we believe we are separate, we start competing with other human beings.

Separateness gives rise to many other illusions. We feel kinship towards our own 'clan,' whether this is our ethnic group, citizens of our country, or members of our religion. We can view members of other communities as inferior or superior to us. Some of the gravest crimes are committed because of the illusion of separateness or disunity. We feel it is okay to mistreat and discriminate against members of other communities because we believe we are separate from them, and they are inferior to us. We would never ill-treat another human being if we understood that we are one with them.

Therefore, created matter veils our true state of oneness and gives rise to beliefs and behaviours that cause pain and suffering. The illusion of disunity gives rise to other illusions, which make our illusory world appear real. It takes a concerted effort to look past the illusion and awaken to our true state.

21

Ataḥ satatam udyuktaḥ spanda-tattva-viviktaye/
Jāgradeva nijaṃ bhāvam acireṇādhigacchati//

Therefore, one should constantly strive to discern the Spanda state. Then, one will quickly attain one's true state even in the waking state.

The Spanda state is the state of awareness. Spanda literally means movement or vibration. However, as explained earlier in this text, Spanda is sometimes used interchangeably with consciousness. It is used to describe consciousness more accurately; to show that consciousness is dynamic and pulsating with life.

Therefore, the Spanda state is a state of awareness. One should constantly strive to be aware. Awareness is the essence of who we are. It is the means by which we awaken from the illusory world. To be aware means to be fully in the present moment. Not even 1% of our attention is elsewhere. We are completely attentive to the present moment. When 100% of our attention is to the present moment, to what life is presenting before us, we break through the illusion and reach our true state. As the *Shiva Sutras* states (3.15): *Attentiveness is the seed.*

To achieve this requires earnest effort. Our thoughts may lead us to the past and the future. When this happens, we have to stop thinking and bring ourselves back to the present moment. Gradually, the gap between thoughts will start increasing. We will spend longer and longer periods in awareness. Being aware brings many benefits. Thoughts disturb us. Awareness and freedom from thoughts bring us great peace. We soon start enjoying the experience of awareness and the peace it brings us. That is the beauty of evolution and higher states of consciousness—we keep experiencing more peace and more joy.

22

Atikruddhaḥ prahṛṣṭo vā kiṃ karomi iti vā mṛśan/
Dhāvan vā yatpadaṃ gacchet tatra spandaḥ pratiṣṭhitaḥ//

Spanda is firmly established when one is excessively angry, exceedingly happy, in a quandary over what to do, or running for one's life. One may go there and step into that state.

There are certain moments in our life when it is easy to establish ourselves in Spanda, or consciousness. Usually, we spend effort trying to be aware. However, in some moments, it is easy to step into that state.

The first occurs when our energy has been awakened. We are either excessively angry, or exceedingly happy. Energy is the same but it can take different forms, such as anger or happiness. The key factor here is to *notice* this energy that has awakened. When you are very angry, and having thoughts of anger or violence, suddenly stop the mind and *be aware*. The excessive state of anger will immediately disappear, and leave you in a state of heightened awareness. The *Vigyan Bhairava Tantra* explains in verse 101:

When strong emotions of desire, anger, greed, infatuation, intoxication or jealousy appear—stop the mind! By doing that, the True Reality underlying those emotions, appears.

Similarly, when you are exceedingly happy, focus on the happiness. The *Vigyan Bhairava Tantra* states in verse 71:

Whenever great joy is obtained, or when joy arises on seeing a friend or relative after a long time, one should meditate on that joy. Then the mind will be absorbed into joy.

Usually, when these moments occur, we focus on the friend and forget about the joy. This verse says, forget the friend and focus on the happiness you are experiencing.

An external event may act as a trigger and cause us to experience a great amount of happiness. When we focus on the intense amount of happiness we are experiencing, it causes an internal reaction in us, and we awaken to a higher level of consciousness.

Emotions are nothing but energy in motion. Anger and happiness are not just emotions but also energy in motion, or energy that has awakened. Energy comes from consciousness. A heightened level of energy means that we are just a step away from a heightened level of consciousness. When we are exceedingly angry or happy, we are very close to a high level of awareness.

There are some situations in life, when the mind on its own falls silent without any effort. This verse describes two of them, when one is in a quandary over what to do, or when one is running for their life. Verse 118 of the *Vigyan Bhairava Tantra* gives further examples:

At the commencement and end of a sneeze, during danger, sorrow, weeping, flight from a battlefield, during curiosity, at the commencement and end of hunger. These states are full of the state of God.

People who have had a gun pulled out on them, or faced a life-threatening situation, have often said that time slowed down, or almost stood still in these moments. In such moments, the mind automatically falls silent. When the mind falls still, the doorway to eternity has been opened. One has to step in and enter the state of consciousness. How does one do this? We do this by *being aware* when these moments occur. When we are aware, the mind disappears completely and we remain in the state of high awareness. If we are not aware, we will miss the golden opportunity these moments present. In a short while, the mind will start functioning again and these moments will pass. Instead, seize these moments when they arise and step into the state of Spanda or consciousness.

23

Yām avasthāṃ samālambya yadayaṃ mama vakṣyati/
Tadavaśyaṃ kariṣye 'ham iti saṃkalpya tiṣṭhati//

After taking hold of that state, and having resolved, "I will certainly do whatever it will say to me," one continues to remain in that state.

When you enter into the state of consciousness, you listen to the wisdom it gives you, and allow it to lead you in your life. The soul has far greater wisdom than the mind. It is like comparing the light of the sun with that of a lamp.

How do you listen to your soul or consciousness? The soul speaks to you through *feelings* and *intuition*. Listen to your feelings or to your gut instinct. There is a lot more intelligence there than you can imagine. Sometimes, an idea or thought may suddenly come into our mind, which can help us resolve a problem we are facing, or take the next step forward in our lives. The greatest of discoveries in this world come through a flash of insight, not through extensive reasoning of the mind. This includes Einstein's Theory of Relativity.

What this verse is asking us to do is to take hold of the state of awareness, and allow it to guide us in our lives. The mind is quiet and we live completely in the present moment. Life becomes simple and easy again. We are only concerned with what life is presenting before us in this moment. There is no thought of the past or the future.

The beautiful thing about being aware is the absence of fear. Fear and anxiety are only present when the mind is active. When the mind is still, there is no fear.

Most spiritual traditions emphasise that the highest source of wisdom is within you. The role of an external Guru is also to point you towards your internal Guru. This is what the verse is gently telling us—to use the wisdom within you. You access this wisdom when the mind is still and you are aware. When you go within, you will find a solution to every problem.

When Buddha was dying, his disciples were concerned that there would be no one to guide them. In the final moments of his life, he gave them the same message. Buddha's last words were *Appo Deepo Bhava*—Be a light unto yourself.

24

Tām āśrityordhvamārgeṇa candrasūryāvubhāvapi/
Sauṣumne 'dhvanyastamito hitvā brahmāṇḍagocaram//

By practicing in that elevated way, both the sun and the moon cease, and energy swiftly rises upwards in the central channel, leaves the body, and enters the field of the universe.

According to yoga, there are 72,000 channels (*nadis*) in the body, through which energy flows. Out of these 72,000 channels, three are important—the right channel (*Pingala Nadi*), the left channel (*Ida Nadi*), and the central channel (*Sushumna*). The sun and moon refer to the right and left channels, respectively. At the moment of liberation, energy ceases to flow in the right and left channels. Instead, the dormant energy situated in Mooladhara chakra, at the base of the central channel, is awakened. This dormant energy, known as kundalini, rises swiftly up the central channel piercing each chakra as it rises. When it reaches the highest chakra, *Sahasrara*, located at the crown of the head, an individual is liberated.

This verse describes what takes place at the moment of liberation. This results from practicing the previous verse. When we enter the state of consciousness and listen to it, we remain in that state. By remaining in the state of consciousness, we become liberated.

25

Tadā tasmin mahāvyomni pralīnaśaśibhāskare/
Sauṣupta-padavan mūḍhaḥ prabuddhaḥ syādanāvṛtaḥ//

Then, in that Great Space, one is reabsorbed into Shiva, which the foolish believe may be like deep sleep but the enlightened is fully awake.

Once the energy passes through the highest chakra, it enters the universe and reunites with Shiva, and an individual becomes one with Shiva. The great Indian mystic, Kabir gave a wonderful example to explain this. He said if you immerse a pot into the sea, the pot would get filled with water. If you raise the top of the pot above the sea, the water in the pot becomes separate from the water in the sea. How do you reunite the water in the pot with that of the sea? You break the pot. The water in the pot then gets reabsorbed into the sea.

When we become liberated, the divine energy within us is awakened, and reunites with the divine energy everywhere (God). Our 'pot', or our sense of individuality, disappears. Some philosophical systems state that this is like falling asleep. However, this verse repudiates that. In the state of enlightenment, there is no loss of consciousness. On the contrary, one is full awake.

26

Tadākramya balaṃ mantrāḥ sarvajñabalaśālinaḥ /
Pravartante 'dhikārāya karaṇānīva dehinām //

Seizing the power of that Spanda, the mantras get endowed with the power of omniscience, and gain the ability to start the creation of matter, like the creation of living creatures.

A mantra is a special type of sound or word, or collection of sounds or words. A mantra may not necessarily mean anything but it contains a certain *Shakti* or power. It has the power to bring about change. Mantras are usually chanted to raise consciousness.

The mantras referred to here are creation mantras—ones that can create matter. In Tantra, there is an elaborate Theory of Creation. There are 36 elements of creation responsible for the creation of our universe and all matter in it. These 36 elements of creation are found in different sounds and mantras. Therefore, all matter is created by certain sounds and mantras, those that contain the elements of creation. The Tantric theory of creation is elaborated on in other texts—*The Malini Vijay Tantra, Paratrishika*, and Abhinavagupta's *Tantraloka* (Light on Tantra).

Today, our scientists are confirming what our ancient mystics told us centuries ago—all matter is created by sounds. Sounds are basically a vibration of energies.

The verse goes one step further. From where do these mantras and elements of creation get their power? Their power comes from Spanda or consciousness. Consciousness is the ultimate power responsible for the creation of matter and life. Mantras gain the power to create life from consciousness. Ultimately, there is only one source of creation, which goes by different names—Shiva, God, consciousness, or Spanda. All life originates from this one source.

27

Tatraiva saṃpralīyante śāntarūpā nirañjanāḥ /
Sahārādhaka-cittena tenaite Śivadharmiṇaḥ //

Because these mantras are endowed with the properties of Shiva, like tranquillity and purity, by reciting them, the mind of the worshipper, along with him, is completely dissolved.

Some mantras contain the properties of Shiva. By reciting them, one is able to still the mind and dissolve the ego, thereby reaching the highest state. The most famous of these mantras is *Aum Namah Shivaya*, which literally means, salutations to Shiva. More importantly, *Aum Namah Shivaya* consists of seven syllables—*Aum*, *na*, *ma*, *h*, *shi*, *va*, *ya*. Each of these syllables stimulates one of the seven chakras and raises our level of consciousness. Another powerful mantra that is chanted is *Shiva Shambo*. It is recommended that *Aum Namah Shivaya* and other mantras are practiced under the guidance of a Guru.

An important point to understand about these mantras is that they are used to dissolve oneself. They do not fulfil a desire of yours, such as getting a promotion in your job, or buying a new house. Instead, they dissolve your ego and bring out your Divine Self.

One of the most powerful mantras for self-realisation is the sound of one's breath. This mantra does not need to be consciously recited. It is automatically recited by a human being 21,600 times, during a day and night. Our breath makes the sound *so* while breathing in and *ham* (pronounce hum), while breathing out. *So* comes from the Sanskrit word *sa*, which means that, and *ham* comes from *aham*, which means I. *So-hum* literally means 'I am That." That is Shiva or God. Therefore, our breath continuously makes the sound, 'I am Shiva,' throughout the day and night.

In the *Vigyan Bhairava Tantra*, Lord Shiva gives 112 meditations for self-realisation. At the end of the text, he gives one final meditation. A meditation, he says, is easy to practice and through which, anyone who is in their senses can obtain success. That meditation is listening to the sound of one's breath.

28

Yasmāt sarvamayo jīvaḥ sarvabhāva-samudbhavāt /
Tatsaṃvedanarūpeṇa tādātmya-pratipattitaḥ //

Any living being arises from the Whole Being, which contains all, and therefore acquires its nature, having the form of consciousness.

All living beings arise from the Whole Being, which is Shiva or God. The Whole Being contains everything, living beings and non-living objects. The basic nature of Shiva or the Whole Being is consciousness. Anything that arises from the Whole Being will acquire its nature, which is consciousness.

Verses 6, 12, and 26 explained to us that consciousness is the power responsible for the creation of life and matter. It is what creates our body and breathes life into it. When consciousness (our soul) leaves our body, our body passes away. Consciousness is responsible for the creation, maintenance, and dissolution of our body.

All matter contains consciousness to some degree. An inanimate object will have less consciousness. Plants have a higher level of consciousness, animals even more so. Finally, humans have the greatest amount of consciousness, and have the ability to be self-aware.

Having self-awareness and a higher level of consciousness means that humans have greater intelligence compared to plants and animal life.

In some science fiction movies, humans battle against intelligent machines for survival. In the recent past, the *Terminator* series and *Matrix* series of movies have used this theme. While these movies are highly entertaining, the reality is that humans can rest easy. Machines, and even apes for that matter, will never pose a threat to us. They simply do not have the level of consciousness, and consequently intelligence, to match wits against humans.

29

Tasmācchabdārthacintāsu na sāvasthā na yā śivaḥ /
Bhoktaiva bhogyabhāvena sadā sarvatra saṃsthitaḥ //

Therefore, on careful thought on the nature of sounds, it is clear that there is no state that is not Shiva. The experiencer, in fact, together with the objects being experienced, always, everywhere, abides in Shiva.

'Sounds' is a reference to all objects, living and non-living, found in this universe. The word 'sounds' has been used to denote objects. In verse 26, it was explained that as per the theory of creation in Tantra, all matter is created by 36 elements of creation, found in certain sounds and mantras. Therefore, the first sentence of the verse is referring to the nature of all objects (created by sound), found in this universe.

As the previous few verses have explained, all objects ultimately arise from the Whole Being, which is Shiva or Consciousness. Shiva or God contains everything. What this means is that you the experiencer, together with every object you are experiencing or interacting with, are always part of Shiva. There is actually no separation between all objects and God. Everything is one; everything is part of the Whole Being. The separation we see between objects in this world is an illusion.

It is important to be aware of certain spiritual laws that govern our existence. We are always using these laws, either consciously or unconsciously. One such law is the Law of Karma or action. The Law of Karma arises from the fact that we are all One and are not separate. The law states that what we do for another, we do for ourselves, and what we fail to do for another, we fail to do for ourselves. If you cheat or hurt someone, someone in the future will cheat or hurt you. All our actions have consequences. What we do to others is done to us. Our acts of love and kindness, or hatred and injustice, only rebound on us. The reason this happens is that there is no separation between us and the other. What we do to another, we are actually doing to ourselves. What we cause another to experience, we will one day experience.

Buddha explained that even if you hide in the middle of the sea, or deep in a cave in the mountains, you couldn't escape the consequences of your actions. Jesus Christ summarised the Law of Karma best when he said, "Do unto others what you would have others do unto you."

30

Iti vā yasya saṃvittiḥ krīḍātvenākhilaṃ jagat /
Sa paśyan satataṃ yukto jīvanmukto na saṃśayaḥ //

Or constantly joined to Consciousness, seeing the world as a play and eager to be Whole. He, who has this perception, is without doubt liberated while still alive.

The previous verse states that we, along with objects being experienced, always abide in Shiva. If we are always one with God, why is it that we do not always experience our oneness with God? And how can we experience our unity with God? The first question is answered later in this text. This verse answers the second question. It gives one method of liberation, or for experiencing our union with Shiva, which is the same thing.

Or constantly joined to Consciousness, seeing the world as a play and eager to be Whole. There are three things that need to be done. One has to be constantly joined to consciousness; one must see the world as a play, and one should be eager to be whole. Eagerness to be whole, or our desire for liberation, is considered to be very important by the author of this text. The next few verses are devoted to this subject.

Being constantly joined to consciousness is not something one is doing; it is something one is being. One is being aware. The most important requirement for liberation is to still the mind. This is a message that keeps coming up. It is one of the central messages of the *Vigyan Bhairava Tantra*, where Lord Shiva tells Parvati that in order to experience the state of God, one has to still the mind. He then proceeds to give 112 meditations for achieving that.

Being constantly joined to consciousness means one is always trying to be aware. If a thought arises, leave it, and return to being aware.

It is important to see the world as a play; otherwise, one will not be able to still the mind. The world can disturb us. Events can arise that disturb us and cause us to start thinking. You lose your job, the stock market crashes, a family member falls seriously ill, and your mind starts racing again. It is important to change our perception and realise that the world is not real. It is like a play, a game, or a movie being played out on the screen of life. We believe the world is real and that is why we experience it as real. This verse is asking us to change our beliefs. Believe the world is not real, and it will no longer trouble you. It does not matter whether we succeed or fail in life, or what our achievements are. Success or failure in your workplace or social circle is of no consequence. Understand that you are simply playing a role in life, not unlike the roles played by actors and actresses in a movie.

When we remain peaceful in the face of a calamity, we are better able to take decisions to improve the external circumstances of our lives. A peaceful mind finds solutions to our problems, whether it is the loss of a job, of wealth, or a family member's illness. On the other hand, an agitated mind does not find the best solutions and only damages our health.

Your real success depends on you seeing the world as a play, and not allowing the dramas of your life to affect you. That is when you achieve *vairagya* or detachment. When you are detached from the world, you can truly enjoy it. With detachment comes peace and equanimity of mind. With equanimity of mind, one reaches the higher levels of awareness, and finally liberation.

The *Shiva Sutras* also emphasises that the world is a play. Sutras 3.9-3.11 state:

The Self is an actor.
The inner self is the stage.
The sense organs are the spectators.

This is a message that God has sent to us through many different people through the ages. In William Shakespeare's *As You Like It*, Jaques says: "All the world's a stage, and all the men and women merely players. They have their exits and their entrances, and one man in his time plays many parts, his acts being seven ages."

31

Ayamevodayas tasya dhyeyasya dhyāyi-cetasi /
Tadātmatā-Samāpattir icchataḥ sādhakasya yā/

This result is, in fact, a consequence of him being intent on consciousness. Realising one's essential state is a product of one's desire for it.

This is the first among many verses on the importance of desire in achieving liberation. To be constantly joined to consciousness, you need to be intent on consciousness. Being conscious, being aware must be a priority in your life, in order for you to achieve it. As Neale Donald Walsch's *Conversations with God, Book 1* states: "Your life proceeds out of your intentions for it." What are your intentions, your desires in life? Life will proceed to bring about fulfilment of your desires.

To be intent on consciousness, you require determination. You have to be able to take your mind off everything else and focus on remaining aware. Ultimately, it is about being determined not to harbour any thoughts. If a thought arises, you witness it and leave it. You give up all concern about the past and future and live totally in the present moment. When not even 1% of your mind is in the past or the future, you become enlightened.

Living in the present moment is wonderful. It is when our mind takes us to the past or the future that we suffer. An event may occur in our life that we deem to be negative. From that our mind will anticipate a series of further negative events, which usually results in us experiencing fear. Fear is the basic emotion we experience when our mind is running our lives and things go wrong. It is impossible to experience sustained periods of happiness when the mind is in control. Happiness comes from peace and peace arises in the absence of thoughts. Thoughts disturb us. Only in the absence of thoughts do we experience peace.

When people start off on the spiritual path, they make an attempt to remain aware and still the mind. Then something goes wrong and they forget all their spiritual practices, and start worrying. Ramana Maharshi gave a beautiful example of how to address this. He explained, when we step on a train, we can put our bag down. The train will take our bag and us to the destination. If we continue carrying our bag, we are only straining ourselves unnecessarily. Similarly, God bears all our burdens and takes care of us. We need to learn to trust God, or the process of life. God takes care of all our needs. If we continue worrying, we are straining ourselves unnecessarily. God or consciousness is the supreme power that bestows life upon all things. This has been explained in the earlier verses. When we are aware, we are constantly in touch with this power. Then, ideas and solutions to our problems appear magically before us.

32

Iyamevāmṛtaprāptir ayamev ātmano grahaḥ /
Iyaṃ nirvāṇa-dīkṣā ca śiva-sadbhāvadāyinī //

This, in fact, is the attainment of the nectar of immortality. This indeed is the realisation of the Self. This is the entry into liberation, which bestows the state of Shiva.

Liberation, or Self-Realisation, brings the state of Shiva. We experience our oneness with God. Liberation in Hinduism is very different from liberation in western religions. Western religions are dualistic. Two exist: the individual and God, and the individual is separate from God. At the end of his or her life, an individual is judged by God, and if found worthy, is admitted into heaven. Liberation in western religions is an entry into heaven.

In the non-dualistic tradition of Kashmir Shaivism, the individual is never separate from God. We *appear* and *feel* separate from Shiva. This is because of the illusion we live in. The illusion conceals true reality and makes us forget our oneness with God. Liberation is nothing but the awakening out of the illusion, or removal of the veil, so that an individual experiences their unity with God. Liberation is the ending of the separateness and of the individual. The individual 'I,' or the ego disappears into the universal Whole.

The *Shiva Sutras* uses the word *kevali* to describe liberation. Kevali literally means alone, only, one. In the liberated state, you realise there is only you; there is only one. Nothing else exists. To put it differently, in the liberated state you are one with God, and experience that only God exists, and nothing other than God exists.

Our beliefs about God influence the way we feel about God. If we believe that we are separate from God, and at the end of our life will be judged by God, then we have reason to fear God. On the other hand, if we believe we are one with God, we will never fear but only love God. We cannot fear ourselves; we can only love ourselves.

33

**Yathecchābhyarthito dhātā jāgrato 'rthān hṛdi sthitān /
Somasūryodayaṃ kṛtvā sampādayati dehinaḥ //**

According to the desire abiding in the heart, God brings about the creation of what has been desired. This is what causes the sun and moon to reach their end, resulting in the awakening of the embodied.

Desire is one of the most important tools of creation. We are creative beings: we do create our own future. We are either doing this consciously or unconsciously. God brings about creation of our deepest desire, the desire residing in our heart.

Our deepest desire also drives us and motivates us in life. As the *Brihad-aranyaka Upanishad* (iv.4.5) puts it so eloquently:

You are what your deep driving desire is.
As your desire is, so is your will.
As your will is, so is your deed.
As your deed is, so is your destiny.

When your deep driving desire is to be liberated, that is what becomes the focus of your life. It drives you to be and do things to achieve your objective. It is what caused the Buddha to leave his family, give up a luxurious life as a prince, and search for a way to be enlightened. It became the sole focus of his life for the next few years, till he became liberated.

This is what causes the sun and moon to reach their end, resulting in the awakening of the embodied. The sun and moon are a reference to the right and left channels, respectively. Usually, our energy is flowing more strongly in one of these channels. This is reflected in the flow of breath in our nostrils. When there is a greater flow of air through our right nostril, it means that there is more energy flowing through the right channel (sun). Similar is the case with the left nostril and the left channel (moon). During a few moments in the day, energy flows through our central channel (located primarily in our spine). At these moments, the flow of breath in both the nostrils is equal. When we are liberated, the dominant energy, kundalini, located at Mooladhara chakra near the base of the spine, is awakened. This energy travels up through the central channel, as described in verse 24. At that moment, energy ceases to flow through the right and left channels. These two channels (sun and moon) reach their end as the verse says.

34

Tathā svapne 'pyabhīṣṭārthān praṇayasyānatikramāt /
Nityaṃ sphuṭataraṃ madhye sthito 'vaśyaṃ prakāśayet //

So, even in the dream state, from a continuous request for one's desire, God, who is always abiding in the centre of oneself, will certainly manifest most vividly the objects that are desired.

Some people may feel that the practical experiences of their life shows that their desires are hardly ever met. They then doubt the power of desire. This usually happens because they frequently change their desire. To manifest a desire quickly, *keep choosing the same thing.* When we frequently change our desire, life keeps changing what it tries to bring us.

By continuously choosing the same desire, God, who is within us, will manifest most clearly what we have desired. We find we suddenly meet the right people, or the right set of circumstances miraculously appears in our life, to help us achieve our goal. There is a saying in spiritualism that is very true—*God is always on our side.* We do not believe this, which is why we are not able to use the creative power of God that resides within us. Sometimes circumstances appear in our life that we do not agree with. We then question, "Why is this happening to me if God is on my side?" All circumstances bring us benefit. Sometimes the benefit is not apparent till years later.

Steve Jobs spoke about this in his commencement address to the Stanford University Class of 2005. He called it connecting the dots. You can only connect the dots looking back in your life. He gave the example of how he dropped out of Reed College because he did not see the point of using up all his parents' savings for a college education he was not sure was going to help him figure out what he wanted to do with his life. Dropping out had some benefits. It allowed him to drop into some classes that he was really interested in, like the excellent calligraphy class they taught at Reed. Ten years later, the value of that calligraphy class became apparent. When he designed the first Macintosh computer, he created the most beautiful typography for it, by using what he had learnt in that calligraphy class. The benefit of dropping out of college, and consequently sitting in on that calligraphy class, became apparent ten years later.

35

Anyathā tu svatantrā syāt sṛṣṭis taddharmakatvataḥ /
Satataṃ Laukikasyeva jāgratsvapnapadadvaye //

Otherwise, one may be giving up the freedom to create, which is the nature of God that is constantly with one, as is the case of ordinary people in both the waking and dream state.

When you do not use the creative power of Shiva, you give up the freedom to create or alter the conditions of your life. All the conditions of our life are subject to change. Which way it is going to change is up to us. Most people do not use the power of desire to alter the conditions of their life. They sometimes see themselves as helpless victims of the circumstances of their life, without realising that everything is subject to change. However, more important than the external condition is the 'inner condition.' Are we allowing external circumstances to affect us? The illusion is just that—an illusion. It is unreal. When we understand this, our entire perspective on the conditions of our life changes. No external event has the power to affect us unless we allow it to. Our inner reaction is completely within our control. That is where the real victory is won. We can choose to be happy no matter what and where we will be. That is when we gain victory over the illusion and enter the state of enlightenment.

Nelson Mandela was imprisoned for 27 years for rising up against the apartheid regime of South Africa. While in jail, he suffered innumerable acts of cruelty. But he never gave into despair, and forgave his captors. He did not allow the circumstances of his life to bring him down. As he famously said:

"I am fundamentally an optimist. Whether that comes from nature or nurture, I cannot say. Part of being optimistic is keeping one's head pointed towards the sun, one's feet moving forward. There were many dark moments when my faith in humanity was sorely tested, but I would not and could not give myself up to despair. That way lays defeat and death."

36

Yathā hi artho 'sphuṭo dṛṣṭaḥ sāvadhāne 'pi cetasi /
Bhūyaḥ sphuṭataro bhāti svabalodyogabhāvitaḥ //

Since initially one's goal manifests unclearly. However, on constant attention of the mind on it, the object is made to manifest most clearly through the continuous exercise of one's power.

The key to manifesting your goal is to focus constantly on it. That is how your desires materialise—through your constant attention on them.

Warren Buffett first met Bill Gates on the weekend of 5 July 1991. At the time, they were the two richest men in the world. They met the owner and editor of the *Washington Post* newspaper, at a weekend holiday on an island off the coast of Seattle. Buffett and Gates were initially sceptical about meeting each other. However, on meeting, they hit it off almost immediately. Buffett skipped the trivial talk and asked Gates about the future prospects of IBM. Gates, in turn, asked Buffett about the economics of the newspaper business. The two of them ended up talking for hours.

Later that evening, over dinner, Gates' father asked everybody a question: "What factor did people feel was the most important in getting to where they had gotten in life?" Buffett answered in one word—"Focus". Gates also gave the same answer.

Both, Warren Buffett and Bill Gates were amongst the most successful men of their generation. They did not discuss other factors, such as intelligence, education, or networking. Instead, they chose to emphasise the importance of focus, which is exactly what this verse and the next verse are stating.

37

Tathā yatparamārthena yena yatra yathā sthitam /
Tattathā balam ākramya na cirāt sampravartate //

So, in reality, remaining focused on the desire is the manner by which desired objects are manifested. Therefore, by seizing that power, one is able to manifest a desire very quickly.

One cannot overstate the importance of being focused on one's objective. It is the single most important factor that will determine whether we achieve our goal or not, and also how quickly we will achieve our objective.

Take the example of two college students. One gets into the best university in the country and the other goes to a lesser known college. However, the one in the lesser known college has a strong desire to succeed and remains focused on that. On the other hand, the student in the better university is not as driven and is more easily distracted. Which student do you think is more likely to succeed in life—the one who is more focused on his goal, but goes to a lesser known college, or the presumably brighter student who went to the best college in the country, but is not so focused? Without doubt it would be the student with a deep desire to succeed, from the lesser known college.

When we are not fully focused on our objective, we become part-time yogis. We are focusing on our liberation and our spiritual practices only part of the time, maybe for a few minutes a day. Progress will then be slow. To improve our pace of progress, we have to spend more time focused on our objective.

The epic, *Mahabharata*, has a beautiful story that illustrates the importance of focus. The great teacher Dronacharya was teaching archery to the Kaurava and Pandava princes. He set up a wooden bird on a tree and asked the princes to knock the bird over by shooting its eye with an arrow, from across the river. The first prince to step forward was Yudhishthira. Dronacharya asked him what he saw. He said, "I see you, my brothers, the river, the tree, and the bird. Dronacharya replied he would fail and asked him to step down. Other princes stepped forward and gave the same answer, much to the disappointment of the teacher. Finally, Arjuna stepped forward and when asked what he saw, he replied, "I only see the eye of the bird." "Then shoot," said Dronacharya, and Arjuna succeeded in knocking the bird down by hitting it in the eye. That is the power of focus.

38

Durbalo 'pi tadākramya yataḥ kārye pravartate /
Ācchādayed bubhukṣāṃ ca tathā yo 'ti bubhukṣitaḥ //

Taking hold of that power, even a weak person can materialise his goal, and in the same way, a person who is very hungry may overcome his hunger.

The creative power of desire is available to everybody because God is in everybody. Even a physically weak and hungry person can overcome his hunger through his desire. We should not make the mistake of believing that the power of desire is only available to the physically strong, or the spiritually evolved amongst us. We can use the power of desire to overcome immediate pressing needs, such as hunger. We can also use this power to overcome our physical limitations.

History has given us many examples of people who have overcome their limitations and gone on to achieve great things. One such person was the German composer Ludwig von Beethoven. He lost most of his hearing at the age of 21. He used the help of various hearing aids. His hearing continued to deteriorate in his 20s and by his last decade, he was almost deaf. He continued to compose great work, and some of his greatest works were completed towards the end of his life. His accomplishments were all the more remarkable, given the fact that he could not hear his own music. He is a fine example of someone who overcame his physical limitations through his strong will and desire, and went on to achieve great success in life.

39

Anenādhiṣṭhite dehe yathā sarvajñatādayaḥ /
Tathā svātmany adhiṣṭhānāt sarvatraivaṃ bhaviṣyati //

Since one achieves this by seizing this power that resides in an individual, therefore, in this way, by abiding in one's own self, one will soon become omniscient for all time.

Seven of the last eight verses focus on the importance of desire. These past verses culminate in the message of this verse—use the power of desire that resides within you to liberate yourself. How does one do this? By choosing to abide in one's own Self. Choose to focus on your Self. Make that your deep driving desire.

To abide in one's own Self is one of the most important ways to achieve liberation. Abiding in one's Self means to be Self-aware, to direct some of our attention back towards our Self. Usually, 100% of our attention is directed outwards. When we direct some of that attention back inwards, we become Self-aware. To be Self-aware means to be in a state of awareness. We become a witness and observe the events of our life, instead of becoming totally lost in them.

Sri Nisargadatta Maharaj was a Self-realised master who lived in Bombay and passed away there in 1981, at the age of 84. People came to meet him from all over the world. He was once asked, "What do you see?" He replied, "I see what you could see, here and now, but for the wrong focus of your attention. You give no attention to your Self. Your mind is all with things, people, and ideas, never with your Self. Bring your Self into focus, become aware of your own existence." (*I Am That: Talks with Sri Nisargadatta Maharaj*).

The Self within us is Shiva. When we focus on the Self, we are focusing on God. Ramana Maharshi also emphasised the importance of abiding in the Self. He said that focusing the mind on the Self is the perfection of yoga, meditation, wisdom, and all forms of spiritual practices. He also went on to say that if we direct our attention outwards to the physical world, we experience pain and anguish. When we direct our attention inwards to the Self, we experience happiness.

Abiding in the Self is a practice that was given in verse 8. It is repeated here again to show how important it is. It is repeated once more, at the end of the book. The *Vigyan Bhairava Tantra* also describes it beautifully:

All contact with pleasure, pain, etc. is through the sense organs. Therefore, one should detach oneself from the senses, turn within and abide in one's own self. (Verse 136).

40

Glānir viluṇṭhikā dehe tasyāścājñānataḥ sṛtiḥ /
Tadunmeṣa-viluptaṃ cet kutaḥ sā syād ahetukā //

Depression of the mind ravages the body and arises due to ignorance. However, if ignorance is destroyed when one awakens, how can depression continue to exist in the absence of its cause?

Most illnesses arise through the mind or through the mouth. Our state of mind and the food we eat is a major contributory factor towards illnesses. The linkage between one's state of mind and diseases was not clear to the medical community till recently. However, yoga and spiritualism knew about this, centuries ago. Now, it is very clear that if we remain tense and anxious for large periods of time, we are likely to suffer from high blood pressure, or diabetes, later in life. Similarly, depression also ravages the body and damages our health.

Depression arises due to ignorance. There is ignorance of the true nature of the world. Equally important is the belief that we need something outside of our self to be happy. We look for happiness outside, in the conditions of our life. The circumstances of our life can sometimes cause unhappiness and even depression. There are stories of billionaires who have committed suicide, when they discovered they had a terminal disease. The onset of a major illness can cause depression. So can the death of a loved one. Sometimes, the absence of a condition can cause depression, such as the lack of success in our lives. We desperately want to achieve success or fame, and when we don't achieve it, we become depressed.

Enlightenment sweeps away our ignorance and our old belief systems. An awakened person realises the world is not real. We are all actors on a stage, like Shakespeare said. We are only playing a role in life. When we make our roles real, we get affected by the conditions of our life and experience pain. Our soul does not care about the successes or failures of the body and neither will you when you awaken. Conditions in life appear to help us evolve. We react to these conditions, judge them, and sometimes experience happiness or unhappiness. However, it is important to remember that we cannot always control the external circumstances of our life, but we can always control our reactions to them. We can choose to be happy, no matter what is happening in the external world, and we will be. The sage Patanjali, in the *Yoga Sutras*, called this state *Pratyahara*, a stage in our evolution when the external world ceases to affect us.

The main point to understand is that we are looking for happiness in the wrong place. We want lasting happiness and we look for it in the external world. But the external world cannot give us lasting happiness; it is a world of change and temporary conditions, where we experience pain alternating with pleasures. True happiness is only found within. When our mind is stilled, we experience bliss. This bliss is far greater than any pleasure the external world can give us. The *Brihad-aranyaka Upanishad* goes to great lengths to explain how if we add up all the pleasures we experience from the external world, they will amount to only a fraction of the joy we experience within us, when we awaken.

With enlightenment, our ignorance is removed, along with our dependence on external conditions for happiness. How can depression then continue, in the absence of its cause?

41

Ekacintāprasaktasya yataḥ syādaparodayaḥ /
Unmeṣaḥ sa tu vijñeyaḥ svayaṃ tam upalakṣayet //

When one is focused on a single thought, there should be the appearance of the Highest State. But to know this fully awakened state, one should experience it for oneself.

When you are focused on a single thought, usually a mantra, other thoughts do not arise and the mind quietens down. That single thought is used to prevent other thoughts from arising. After a certain stage, when the mind becomes stable, that single thought is also not required. It is discarded, the mind is perfectly still, and then there is the appearance of the Highest State.

The single thought may be a mantra, usually given by a Guru. Certain mantras work on the restless mind and induce it to become still. The mantra may or may not have any meaning. It is the sound of the mantra that works on the mind and makes it tranquil. Yoga is like a science. It is the science of liberation. It uses sounds (mantras), it uses diagrams (mandalas), and a variety of other tools to help an individual achieve self-realisation.

The fully awakened state cannot be described accurately using the words of our language. That is why the words of a master are sometimes misunderstood. It is because they are using words to describe experiences that cannot easily be communicated in words. To know the liberated state, one has to experience it for oneself.

Lord Shiva says something similar in the *Vigyan Bhairava Tantra.* The Goddess asks him about the liberated state. He doesn't answer her directly. Instead, he gives her 112 meditations for self-realisation. What he is trying to tell her is this—to know the liberated state fully, you need to experience it for yourself. Here are 112 meditations to help you reach that state.

42

Ato vindur ato nādo rūpam asmād ato rasaḥ /
Pravartante 'cireṇaiva kṣobhakatvena dehinaḥ //

From this state, very soon arises the dot, from this sound, from this form, from this taste, with shaking of the body.

From this state refers to the beginning of the last verse—when you are focused on a single thought, the mind has become still, and you are about to awaken. At the moment of liberation, or shortly before it, you may undergo some mystical experiences. You may see a dot, or a point of light, between your eyebrows. This dot of light is your soul. After this, you may hear supernatural sounds. There are ten sounds that sages have reported hearing:

a) The sound of a bee humming.
b) The sound of the word C*hini*.
c) The sound of bells ringing.
d) The sound of a conch shell.
e) The sound of a stringed instrument or a veena.
f) The sound of cymbals.
g) The sound of a flute.
h) The sound of a drum echoing.
i) The sound of two drums.
j) Finally, the sound of thunder.

You may also visualise some forms, or experience the taste of nectar on your tongue. The *Svetasvatara Upanishad* lists the forms that appear before final liberation: a mist, smoke, and a sun; wind, fireflies, and a fire; lightnings, a clear crystal, and a moon.

Finally, you may experience trembling or shaking of the body. This is the moment that kundalini has awakened, and is rising from the base chakra through your spine, to the topmost chakra. The moment it pierces the highest chakra, you are liberated.

43

Didṛkṣayeva sarvārthān yadā vyāpyāvatiṣṭhate /
Tadā kiṃ bahunoktena svayameva avabhotsyate //

When through his desire for seeing Reality, he perceives himself absorbed in and permeating everything, then why say much? He will experience it for himself.

Vasugupta once again touches on the experience of enlightenment. Through one's desire for liberation, one reaches the liberated state. In that state, one experiences oneness with everything. You realise that only you exist. Everything is part of you. Nothing other than you exists. You permeate and are absorbed in everything. Beyond this, Vasugupta does not say much. He says you will experience it for yourself.

Other ancient Indian texts have gone into a little more detail about the experience of enlightenment. The *Isha Upanishad* states:

He who sees all beings in his Self and his Self in all beings, thereafter has no fear.

The wise man for whom all beings have actually become one with his Self; then what delusion and what sorrow can exist for him, after seeing this oneness?

The *Brihad-aranyaka Upanishad* describes enlightenment thus:

Where there seems to be another, there one may see another, one may smell another, one may taste another, one may speak to another, one may hear another, one may think about another, one may touch another and one may know another.

But when one becomes clear like water, the Seer is alone and there is no other.

44

Prabuddhaḥ sarvadā tiṣṭhej jñānenālokya gocaram /
Ekatrāropayet sarvaṃ tato 'nyena na pīḍyate //

Beholding the sensory world with knowledge, one should always remain awake and should attribute everything to one Source. Then, one is not troubled by another.

On the way to enlightenment, how does one live in the world we experience through our senses? We live in this world with right knowledge; with our understanding that what we are seeing is not real. We see a world with diversity, separation, and disunity. But our sense organs cannot show us the underlying unity of all the different objects we see and experience. Like Alice in

Wonderland, we live in a world where things are not what they seem.

One should also try and remain awake. Awake here is meant in a deeper sense. It is not referring to the waking state but to a state of awareness. We should try and remain aware and keep the mind still.

There is a word used in this verse, *Ekatra*, which literally means, *in one, in one place, in one and the same place.* It has been translated here as "one Source". We are to attribute everything in this world to one Source, one place, one Self, or one God. When we do this, we are not troubled by another person or event. Sometimes, a person in our life may trouble us. The way to remain undisturbed by another is to realise that we all spring from the same Source and are not separate from each other. We are one with the person disturbing us.

A person has entered our lives because God has put them there. People enter into our lives for a reason: they are there to help us evolve. Even the ones who trouble us are there for the same reason—to help us move forward in our evolution. It is the same with events. They all appear for a reason. Sometimes, that reason is not apparent till years later. To remain undisturbed by people and events, we need to change our perception. Life is perfection playing itself out. Whatever happens actually happens for the best. People enter and exit our lives at the right moment. Play the game of life and understand that nothing is real. You have no reason to fear a world which is unreal.

45

Śabdarāśi-samutthasya śaktivargasya bhogyatām /
Kalāvilupta-vibhavo gataḥ san sa paśuḥ smṛtah //

The greatness of his true nature disappears because of the forces of concealment, and he becomes a victim of the group of energies appearing as a collection of sounds, and he is known as bound.

How do we forget the greatness of our true nature? What causes this to happen? Our true nature is hidden by the forces of concealment. This is explained in the Theory of Creation in Tantra. This was touched upon briefly in the commentary to verse 26.

From Param Shiva or Supreme God, 36 elements are created. These 36 elements are responsible for the creation of the entire universe, and all matter on it. The first five elements that appear are known as the pure elements. Following these, seven pure-impure elements emerge. Of this group, the first six elements (elements six to eleven) are the forces of concealment referred to in the verse.

The first of these (element 6) is *Maya*, which means illusion. Maya conceals the unity of existence, and causes us to experience separation. We are made to feel separate from other objects and not one with them. Instead of oneness, we experience diversity.

Maya works through the next five elements, elements 7 to 11, which are collectively called *Kanchuka*. Kanchuka means cover. These elements emerge from Maya and veil our real nature.

Element 7 is *Kalaa*. It limits the identification from the Supreme Being to the limited individual; from the Universal Self to the small self. Instead of identifying with consciousness, we identify with the body, or with the name and form.

The next element is *vidya* or knowledge. Vidya reduces us from the state of omniscience to limited knowledge. Element 9 is *Raga* or attraction. Because we feel separate from other objects, there arises attraction for some of them. Without the feeling of separation, there can be no attraction. You cannot be attracted to something that is not separate from you.

The next element is *Kaala* or time. Kaala reduces the eternity of consciousness to the past, present, and future.

Instead of experiencing the eternal, we experience time measured in seconds, minutes, hours, days, weeks, etc.

Finally, element 11 is *Niyati*. Niyati causes us to experience restriction in space and form. Instead of experiencing the all-pervasiveness of our true nature, we experience ourselves in a particular space and form.

These elements are the forces of concealment that cover our true nature.

46

Parāmṛtarasāpāyas tasya yaḥ pratyayodbhavaḥ /
Tenāsvatantratām eti sa ca tanmātragocaraḥ //

Going into the sensory world made of subtle elements, beliefs arise which cause the taste of Supreme Immortality to vanish, and with that he loses his freedom.

The single most important belief that causes us to lose sight of our immortal nature is the belief that, "I am the body." It is caused by Kaala, one of the elements of concealment mentioned in the previous verse. When we see the sensory world, we look at all the different objects that seem separate from us. Each object has a definite boundary. Most objects, or living beings, have a birth and death that is different from us. For example, a parent or friend of ours may pass away, while we are still alive. All this causes us to believe that we are separate from other objects, and we are our body.

Verses 14, 15, and 16 explained to us that this is not true. We are not our body; we are our soul, which is none other than the witnessing Self within us.

In order to realise our true nature, we need to destroy our belief that we are the body. The *Shiva Sutras*, Chapter 2, verses 8–10 explains:

8. The body is the sacrifice. (The physical body is not sacrificed but the idea that I am the body.)

9. Knowledge is food to be consumed. (The limited knowledge that I am the body is to be destroyed.)

10. On destruction of this knowledge, one awakens from experiencing the dream state.

47

**Svarūpāvaraṇe cāsya śaktayaḥ satatotthitāḥ /
Yataḥ śabdānuvedhena na vinā pratyayodbhavaḥ //**

Moreover, these energies are always ready to conceal one's real nature, because without obstruction by sounds, no beliefs can arise.

The second part of the verse needs a little explaining: **because without obstruction by sounds, no beliefs can arise.** How do sounds cause obstruction and allow incorrect beliefs to arise?

In Sanskrit, there is a common word, *Shabd*, used for both sound and word. It was explained earlier that 36 elements are responsible for the creation of the entire universe. These elements work through sound in creating matter. Kashmir Shaivism explains that the elements are found in the energy of sound, specifically in the letters of the Sanskrit alphabet and certain creation mantras. From the sounds of the different Sanskrit letters, the entire universe is created.

All objects, living or inanimate, are therefore created by certain sounds, which contain the 36 elements. These objects, as explained in the previous verse, cause us to identify with and believe we are the body. Because we see other objects that are separate from us, the belief arises that we are the body. So, the second part of the verse is stating that because of obstruction by objects, incorrect beliefs are arising. And because objects are created by sound, it is ultimately sound that is causing the incorrect beliefs to arise. You might find it easier to understand this verse if you substitute the word 'objects' for 'sounds'—**because, without obstruction by objects, no beliefs can arise.**

48

Seyaṃ kriyātmikā śaktiḥ śivasya paśuvartinī /
Bandhayitrī Svamārgasthā jñātā siddhyupapādikā //

The energy of Shiva, having the nature of doing, resides in the bound individual, and causes bondage. But when it is understood that it stands in the way of realising one's own nature, it brings about complete liberation.

The body is always doing something. The energy of doing binds us because we believe, "I am the doer." This belief springs from the fact that we identify with and believe we are the body. The body does things. I am the body and, therefore, I am the one doing all these tasks. As explained in the previous verses, this belief that we are the body prevents us from realising our true nature.

The way out of this is to believe that we are the Self or Consciousness. This way, the energy of doing no longer binds us but can liberate us. The actions of the body are seen as tasks performed by the body, not something done by us. We are the Self or the witness who observes all the actions of the body, and in whose presence the body performs various activities. But we are not the doer ourselves. Ramana Maharshi explains this very clearly:

"*Sannyasa* or renunciation is not the discarding of external things but of the ego."

He then continues to explain:

"As the activities of the sage exist only in the eyes of others and not in his own, although he may be accomplishing immense tasks, he really does nothing. Therefore, his activities do not stand in the way of inaction and peace of mind. For, he knows the truth that all activities take place in his mere presence and that he does nothing. Hence, he will remain as the silent witness of all the activities taking place."

When there is identification with the Self and not the body, there is no sense of being the doer. The energy of doing no longer stands in the way of one experiencing their true state.

49

Tanmātrodaya-rūpeṇa mano 'haṃ-buddhivartinā /
Puryaṣṭakena saṃruddhastaduttham pratyayodbhavam //

Due to the appearance of the body, consisting of the five subtle elements, one believes that they are the body. Identifying with the eight constituent parts of the body hinders the appearance of one's true state. The existence of this belief . . .

50

Bhuṅkte paravaśo bhogaṃ tadbhāvāt saṃsared ataḥ /
Saṃsṛti-pralayasyāsya kāraṇaṃ saṃpracakṣmahe //

. . . causes one to become subservient to sensory pleasures. For this reason, one experiences a mundane existence. Now, we will explain the means for ending this mundane existence.

Finally, what was hinted at in some of the past few verses is stated clearly here. Due to the appearance of the body, one believes they are the body. This belief prevents the appearance of our real state.

Believing we are the body causes us to chase after sensory pleasures and become subservient to them. Our whole life is concerned about seeking pleasure and avoiding pain. Good food, sex, fine clothes, travel, material goods, and the pleasures money can buy become a priority in our lives. That is why the acquisition of money becomes important. We believe through money we can live comfortably and enjoy many different pleasures.

Tantra explains that seeking pleasures and trying to avoid pain is futile and leads to a life of suffering. Life is a cycle; pain follows pleasures just as night follows day. To have one and not the other is impossible.

The *Katha Upanishad* explains that there two paths an individual is attracted to: the path of joy and the path of pleasure. Those who follow the path of pleasure do not reach the other shore. It goes on to explain that pleasures are transient, and the wise do not seek the eternal in things that pass away. The path of joy leads to eternal bliss, but the path of pleasure leads to a mundane existence, as the verse states.

The second part of verse 45 can be better understood now:

. . . and he becomes a victim of the group of energies appearing as a collection of sounds, and he is known as bound.

Instead of sounds, you can substitute the word objects, as explained earlier. What are the group of energies referred to here? They are lust, anger, greed, jealousy, hatred and, above all, desire. We experience these energies when we believe we are the body and feel we are separate from other bodies or objects. The feeling of separation gives rise to all these emotions, and causes us to experience a mundane existence.

So how does one end a life of suffering and experience the bliss of our true nature? The next verse shows one very important method of doing so.

51

Yadā tvekatra saṃrūḍhas tadā tasya layodayau /
Niyacchan bhoktṛtām eti tataścakreśvaro bhavet //

Now, when one is firmly rooted in one's Self, there is disappearance of the individual and the appearance of one's true state. With the mind under control, one enjoys the experiences of life, and then one becomes Lord of the circle of energies.

Focus on the Self. Be aware of the Self. Be a witness. Live in the present moment. Direct your attention inwards.

These and similar messages are repeated by many different masters, from different traditions, who lived in different time periods, sometimes centuries apart. What is remarkable is how similar these messages are. The book ends with a very important method of achieving liberation—be aware of the Self. It is a message that was given in verses 8 and 39. The Self is God. It is being repeated here to show just how important it is. If you have to take only one learning from this book, it would be this: remain aware of the Self.

To be aware of the Self means to be a witness; to remain aware of the witness within us. It means simply to live in the present moment. When our attention is 100% in the present, and there is not even a small part of us in the past or future, then we reach our true state.

Being aware of the breath is another way of focusing on the Self. Listen to the sound of your breath. You can do this anytime during the day, when you have time with yourself.

An important saint in the history of Kashmir Shaivism is the 14th century poetess, Lal Ded, sometimes known as Lalla. She was fully self-realised, and her poetry gives us insights into the Divine. Her message was strikingly similar to this text. Here are three selections from the wonderful translation by Ranjit Hoskote:

41. Focus on the Self.
That's the best advice you can get.

95. My Master gave me just one rule:
Forget the outside, get to the inside of things.
I, Lalla, took that teaching to heart.
From that day, I've danced naked.

104. The Self that lives in you and others:
that's Shiva. Get the measure of Shiva.

The second part of the verse refers to the time after liberation. One's mind is under control, one enjoys the various experiences of life, the peaks along with the valleys, and pleasure and pain no longer affect one. The circle of energies is the chakras. One becomes Lord of the chakras and of all energies; one becomes Shiva himself.

When you remain focused on the Self, you are in touch with the source of all life, and everything about you will be beautiful.

52

Agādhasaṃśayāmbhodhi-samuttaraṇatāriṇīm /
Vande vicitrārthapadāṃ citrāṃ tāṃ gurubhāratīm //

I revere the wonderful speech of my Guru, whose words have beautiful meanings. They are like a boat that enables one to cross the deep ocean of doubt.

Now we have reached the end of the journey. The passage to the other shore has been explained to us. These words are like a boat; they take us from self-doubt to self-realisation, from suffering and pain to eternal bliss. Here are a few of the important messages of this text: Desire is a very important tool for achieving one's objective. Use it, especially for becoming enlightened. Focusing on the Self is one of the surest ways to enlightenment. The appearance of the body, and of other objects, causes us to believe we are the body, and that we are separate from other objects. These beliefs prevent us from experiencing our true nature. We are not the body but the Self. The Self is Shiva. It is the part of God that is within each of us.

53

Labdhvāpy alabhyam etaj jñānadhanaṃ
hṛdguhāntakṛtanihiteḥ /
Vasuguptavac chivāya hi bhavati sadā sarvalokasya //

One should seize this wealth of knowledge, though difficult to obtain, that is placed hidden in the interior of the heart, and will always be for the benefit of all beings. Then, like Vasugupta, one will certainly go to Shiva.

There is some doubt as to whether this verse is part of the original *Spanda Karikas.* Kshemaraja has it in his commentary, but the other ancient commentaries do not mention it in their texts. Some scholars believe this verse may have been added by Kshemaraja, the main disciple of Abhinavagupta.

The *Spanda Karikas* is a remarkable little text. In a little over 50 verses, it imparts a wealth of wisdom. Use the wisdom and become enlightened! In one of her poems, Lalla explains, it is easy to study spiritual texts; it is tougher to look for the Self. Initially, focusing on the Self requires effort. The more one does it, the easier it becomes. Increasingly, as you experience the peace within, the less you are inclined towards turning your attention outwards, away from the Self.

May you have success in your spiritual journey and reunite with God! That is what the *Spanda Karikas* wishes for all of us.

BIBLIOGRAPHY

Byrom, Thomas. *The Heart of Awareness—A Translation of the Ashtavakra Gita.* Boston: Shambhala, 1990, 2001.

Chaudhri, Ranjit. *112 Meditations for Self Realization: Vigyan Bhairava Tantra.* India: Prakash Books India Pvt. Ltd., 2011.

Chaudhri, Ranjit. *The Shiva Sutras: Eternal Wisdom for Life.* India: Prakash Books India Pvt. Ltd., 2019.

Chopra, Deepak. *The Seven Spiritual Laws of Success.* New Delhi: Excel Books, 1996, 2000.

Dyczkowski, Mar S.G. *The Stanzas on Vibration.* USA: State University of New York Press, 1992.

Hoskote, Ranjit. *I, Lalla, The Poems of Lal Ded.* India: Penguin Books India, 2011, 2013.

Maharaj, Sri Nisargadatta. *I Am That.* India: Chetana (P) Ltd., 1973, 2003.

Maharshi, Sri Ramana. *Words of Grace.* Tiruvannamalai: Sri Ramanasramam, 1969, 1996.

Mascaro, Juan. *The Bhagavad Gita.* England: Penguin Books Ltd., 1962, 1994.

Nsehe, Mfonobong. 19 Inspirational Quotes from Nelson Mandela – Forbes. December 6, 2013. https://www.forbes.com/sites/.../2013/.../20-inspirational-quotes-from-nelson-mandela/

Mascaro, Juan. *The Upanishads.* England: Penguin Books Ltd., 1965, 1981.

Mukherjee, Radhakamal. *Astavakragita* (The Song of the Self Supreme). India: Motilal Banarsidass Publishers Private Limited, 1971, 2000.

Radhakrishnan, S. *The Principal Upanishads.* India: Harper Collins Publishers India, 1994, 1997.

Sadhguru. *Himalayan Lust.* Mumbai: Jaico Publishing House, 2010, 2016.

Saraswati, Swami Niranjanananda. *Tantra Darshan.* Munger, India: Yoga Publications Trust, 2013.

Schroeder, Alice. *The Snowball, Warren Buffett and the Business of Life.* Great Britain: Bloomsbury Publishing Plc, 2008.

Singh, Jaideva. *Spanda Karikas.* Delhi: Motilal Banarsidass Publishers Pvt. Ltd., 1980, 2000.

Singh, Jaideva. *Parātrīśikā – Vivaraṇa.* Delhi: Motilal Banarsidass Publishers Pvt. Ltd., 1988, 2002.

Text of Steve Jobs' Commencement Address (2005) – Stanford News. 14 June 2005. https://news.stanford.edu/2005/06/14/jobs-061505/

Venkataramiah, Mungala. *Talks with Sri Ramana Maharshi.* Tiruvannamalai: Sri Ramanasramam, 1955, 2000.

Walsch, Neale Donald. *Conversations with God Book 1, An Uncommon Dialogue.* Great Britain: Hodder and Stoughton, 1997.

Walsch, Neale Donald. *Friendship with God, An Uncommon Dialogue.* Great Britain: Hodder and Stoughton, 1999.

Walsch, Neale Donald. *Communion with God, An Uncommon Dialogue.* Great Britain: Hodder and Stoughton, 2000.

THE VERSES

1) We praise that Shiva, who is the source of all energy existing everywhere, and by whose opening and closing of eyes, the universe is created or destroyed.
2) In whom this whole world rests and from whom it has come, cannot be restrained anywhere, as its nature is open.
3) That which is undivided extends even into the division appearing in the waking state, etc. because one who is aware does not leave their own natural state.
4) "I am happy, I am pained, I am satisfied." These and other feelings evidently abide in another place, where the states of pleasure, pain, etc. are strung together.
5) Where there is neither pain nor pleasure, neither object nor subject, and nor is there also unconsciousness, that is the highest truth.
6) From where does this group of sense organs, along with the inner chakras that are lifeless, become conscious of their own, and what is responsible for their creation, maintenance, and destruction?
7) One should examine carefully with effort, and grasp that element, which by virtue of its natural freedom existing everywhere, is responsible for this.

8) An individual cannot set a desire in motion on their own. But only by being in contact with the power of the Self, one is able to do this. One should become identical to the Self.
9) An individual is incapable of fulfilling their desires because of their impurities. When the agitation of the mind ceases, then one will enter the Highest State.
10) Then the real nature of this one is established, whose very quality is knowledge and activity. Due to this, one is then able to know and do everything one desires.
11) How can he, who looks with astonishment at his natural state, which presides over everything, continue in this selfish way?
12) Non-existence cannot be the state of being to strive for, as there is no consciousness and no existence there. Only from being in constant contact with consciousness can there be existence. This is for certain.
13) For this reason that artificial state is to be understood as similar to being continuously in deep sleep. However, the real state is not remembered as occurring in this way.
14) Two are found to exist here, called the Creator and the created. Among them, created matter is subject to decay but the Creator is imperishable.

15) Looking at created matter dissolving into the Whole, examine carefully what is being destroyed here. At the time of his death, an ignorant man thinks, "I will cease to exist."

16) But the Being within us, who is the abode of the quality of omniscience, cannot be destroyed. Due to lack of knowledge of his other Self, a man believes, sooner or later, he may cease to exist.

17) A fully enlightened person is constantly aware of his Self in the three transitory states. But others may find their Being at the beginning and end of these states.

18) The all-pervading Lord, through the supreme power he possesses, appears in the form of knowledge and objects of knowledge, in the waking state and dream state. But other than these states, God appears as pure Consciousness.

19) Creation of matter, beginning with the qualities, issues from vibration that is connected to the universal vibration of Consciousness. From not standing in the way of knowing this, people may be able to permanently realise their true Self.

20) However, these created matter are active in concealing one's true state and cause the unawakened to fall into the painful path of world illusion, which is difficult to overcome.

21) Therefore, one should constantly strive to discern the Spanda state. Then, one will quickly attain one's true state even in the waking state.

22) Spanda is firmly established when one is excessively angry, exceedingly happy, in a quandary over what to do, or running for one's life. One may go there and step into that state.

23) After taking hold of that state, and having resolved, "I will certainly do whatever it will say to me," one continues to remain in that state.

24) By practicing in that elevated way, both the sun and the moon cease, and energy swiftly rises upwards in the central channel, leaves the body, and enters the field of the universe.

25) Then, in that Great Space, one is reabsorbed into Shiva, which the foolish believe may be like deep sleep but the enlightened is fully awake.

26) Seizing the power of that Spanda, the mantras get endowed with the power of omniscience, and gain the ability to start the creation of matter, like the creation of living creatures.

27) Because these mantras are endowed with the properties of Shiva, like tranquillity and purity, by reciting them, the mind of the worshipper, along with him, is completely dissolved.

28) Any living being arises from the Whole Being,

which contains all, and therefore acquires its nature, having the form of consciousness.

29) Therefore, on careful thought on the nature of sounds, it is clear that there is no state that is not Shiva. The experiencer, in fact, together with the objects being experienced, always, everywhere, abides in Shiva.

30) Or constantly joined to Consciousness, seeing the world as a play and eager to be Whole. He, who has this perception, is without doubt liberated while still alive.

31) This result is, in fact, a consequence of him being intent on consciousness. Realising one's essential state is a product of one's desire for it.

32) This, in fact, is the attainment of the nectar of immortality. This indeed is the realisation of the Self. This is the entry into liberation, which bestows the state of Shiva.

33) According to the desire abiding in the heart, God brings about the creation of what has been desired. This is what causes the sun and moon to reach their end, resulting in the awakening of the embodied.

34) So, even in the dream state, from a continuous request for one's desire, God, who is always abiding in the centre of oneself, will certainly manifest most vividly the objects that are desired.

35) Otherwise, one may be giving up the freedom to create, which is the nature of God that is constantly with one, as is the case of ordinary people in both the waking and dream state.

36) Since initially one's goal manifests unclearly. However, on constant attention of the mind on it, the object is made to manifest most clearly through the continuous exercise of one's power.

37) So, in reality, remaining focused on the desire is the manner by which desired objects are manifested. Therefore, by seizing that power, one is able to manifest a desire very quickly.

38) Taking hold of that power, even a weak person can materialise his goal, and in the same way, a person who is very hungry may overcome his hunger.

39) Since one achieves this by seizing this power that resides in an individual, therefore, in this way, by abiding in one's own self, one will soon become omniscient for all time.

40) Depression of the mind ravages the body and arises due to ignorance. However, if ignorance is destroyed when one awakens, how can depression continue to exist in the absence of its cause?

41) When one is focused on a single thought, there should be the appearance of the Highest State.

But to know this fully awakened state, one should experience it for oneself.

42) From this state, very soon arises the dot, from this sound, from this form, from this taste, with shaking of the body.

43) When through his desire for seeing Reality, he perceives himself absorbed in and permeating everything, then why say much? He will experience it for himself.

44) Beholding the sensory world with knowledge, one should always remain awake and should attribute everything to one Source. Then, one is not troubled by another.

45) The greatness of his true nature disappears because of the forces of concealment, and he becomes a victim of the group of energies appearing as a collection of sounds, and he is known as bound.

46) Going into the sensory world made of subtle elements, beliefs arise which cause the taste of Supreme Immortality to vanish, and with that he loses his freedom.

47) Moreover, these energies are always ready to conceal one's real nature, because without obstruction by sounds, no beliefs can arise.

48) The energy of Shiva, having the nature of doing, resides in the bound individual, and causes bondage.

But when it is understood that it stands in the way of realising one's own nature, it brings about complete liberation.

49) Due to the appearance of the body, consisting of the five subtle elements, one believes that they are the body. Identifying with the eight constituent parts of the body hinders the appearance of one's true state. The existence of this belief . . .

50) . . . causes one to become subservient to sensory pleasures. For this reason, one experiences mundane existence. Now, we will explain the means for ending this mundane existence.

51) Now, when one is firmly rooted in one's Self, there is disappearance of the individual and the appearance of one's true state. With the mind under control, one enjoys the experiences of life, and then one becomes Lord of the circle of energies.

52) I revere the wonderful speech of my Guru, whose words have beautiful meanings. They are like a boat that enables one to cross the deep ocean of doubt.

53) One should seize this wealth of knowledge, though difficult to obtain, that is placed hidden in the interior of the heart, and will always be for the benefit of all beings. Then, like Vasugupta, one will certainly go to Shiva.

About the Author

Ranjit Chaudhri has translated some important texts of Kashmir Shaivism from Sanskrit into English. These include *112 Meditations for Self Realization: The Vigyan Bhairava Tantra*, *The Shiva Sutras: Eternal Wisdom for Life*, and *Sounds of Liberation: The Spanda Karikas*. He presently lives in Kolkata.